Amazing
Animal Journeys

by Alix Wood

WINDMILL BOOKS

New York

Published in 2013 by Windmill Books,
An Imprint of Rosen Publishing
29 East 21st Street, New York, NY 10010

Editor for Alix Wood Books: Mark Sachner
US Editor: Sara Antill
Designer: Alix Wood
Consultant: Sally Morgan

Photo Credits: Cover, 1, 2, 3, 4, 5, 6, 7, 8, 9, 10, 11, 12, 13, 14, 15 (top), 16 (bottom), 17, 18, 19, 20, 21
(bottom), 22, 23 © Shutterstock; 15 (bottom) © U.S. Fish and Wildlife Service; 16 (top) © Frances Whitfield;
21 (top) © Lukas Kurtz

Library of Congress Cataloging-in-Publication Data

Wood, Alix.
 Amazing animal journeys / by Alix Wood.
    p. cm. — (Wow! wildlife)
 Includes index.
 ISBN 978-1-4488-8099-7 (library binding) — ISBN 978-1-4488-8163-5 (pbk.) —
 ISBN 978-1-4488-8170-3 (6-pack)
 1. Animal migration—Juvenile literature. I. Title.
 QL754.W66 2013
 591.56'8—dc23

                    2012001606

Manufactured in the United States of America

CPSIA Compliance Information: Batch #B1S12WM: For Further Information contact Windmill Books, New York, New York at 1-866-478-0556

Contents

What Is Migration?

Migration is the regular long-distance journey by animals from one place to another. Animals migrate to survive. If the food runs out, or the rains haven't come, animals must move to a new area to find food and water. Often these patterns follow the seasons.

Some animals migrate to search for a mate or to have their young. Some migrate due to overcrowding, like the desert locust, below. They form huge **swarms** and migrate long distances to find new feeding grounds.

Impala search for water in a dried-up river bed. They will need to find water to survive.

4

At least 4,000 species of birds migrate. That's about 40 percent of the world's total. In the cold north, lots of birds go south to escape winter. In Europe, about half the species migrate, especially those that eat insects and can't find enough food during winter. In warmer regions, like the Amazon rain forest, not many migrate, as the weather and food are reliable year-round.

WOW! Natural Map Skills

How do they know the way? Animals find their route in a number of ways. Some use landmarks or guide themselves by the stars and the Sun. Smells, tastes, and sounds can help some species find their way. Sea creatures notice changes in the water quality and wave patterns. Some creatures can even sense tiny changes in Earth's magnetic field.

A Long Flight

Many birds migrate. Natural signs, like the changing length of the days, make **hormones** in their bodies tell them to migrate. The hormones make birds behave differently. They eat more. They start flying around and gathering in groups.

The ruby-throated hummingbird is tiny. It's body is about 3 inches (7.6 cm) long, and it weighs about the same as a penny! This amazing hummingbird migrates 500 miles (800 km) nonstop across the Gulf of Mexico!

It's a long, dangerous journey across the Gulf of Mexico. At 25 miles an hour (40 km/h) it is about 20 hours of nonstop flying! Strong winds could blow the birds backward. Their energy could run out. Some hummingbirds fly an easier but longer route across land.

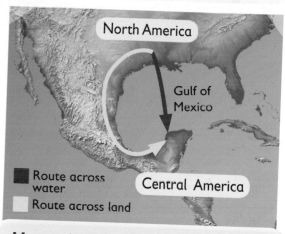

North America

Gulf of Mexico

Central America

■ Route across water
□ Route across land

Hummingbird Migration Routes

WOW! Flying Skills

Hummingbirds' wings can move in a circle. They can fly forward and backward, and they can hover. Their wings beat about 55 times a second when hovering! You try it!

Hummingbirds have to eat a lot before migration. They nearly double their weight.

Choosing the Route

Most birds follow landmarks like rivers or coastlines. Some fly in a straight line, even if this means crossing dangerous stretches of desert or sea.

Many migrating birds go back the same way they came, but some fly in a big **loop**.

Every year, sandhill cranes migrate more than 2,000 miles (3,200 km) south for the winter. These cranes are as tall as a person and have a huge **wingspan**. They use hot rising air to soar in the sky for hours, only flapping their wings now and then.

Sandhill cranes like to dance and jump!

 **Wind Power**

When the wind is against them, birds stick closer to the ground, where hills, trees, and buildings slow the wind down. With the wind blowing behind them, they fly up high. There, the wind will whisk them along faster.

Flying into the wind is tiring.

Sandhill cranes run into the wind to get air under their wings to help them take off. Taking off is the most tiring part of flying.

Bird Freeways

Many migrating birds follow similar routes. These migration routes are called **flyways**. Usually they will have food stops and shelter along the way.

Snow geese spend more than half the year on their migration.

Large flocks of lesser snow geese fly along the Central Flyway. The Central Flyway follows the Great Plains in the United States into Canada. There are no mountains or large hills to fly across. There is water and food all the way.

The Central Flyway

House martins spend summer in Europe and winter in Africa. They migrate across the Mediterranean Sea and the Sahara Desert! They catch their food in the air and hardly ever land on the ground.

Europe

Mediterranean Sea

Sahara Desert

Africa

House Martin Migration Route

House martins gathering on cables in the fall, ready to migrate

WOW! Super Senses

The movement of wind or sea against land makes a low sound the human ear can't hear. Migrating birds use these sounds to "hear" the landscape long before they can see it. They may also be able to smell distant land or water.

Following the Rains

In Africa, many large mammals follow rainfall in a large circular loop each year. Over one million wildebeests and hundreds of thousands of zebras and gazelles follow the same migration route, searching for water and **grazing**.

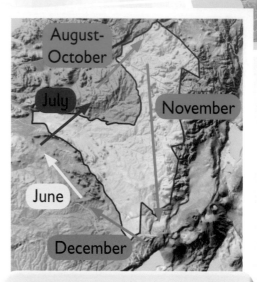

Africa

August-October

July

November

June

December

Wildebeest migration around the Serengeti National Park

A hungry crocodile lies in wait in the Mara River.

These wildebeests and zebras must cross the Mara River. The wide, fast river washes some away. Crocodiles hide at the crossing point and attack the wildebeests as they try to swim across.

WOW! Clever Baby!

A wildebeest calf can stand and run within a few minutes of birth. In a few days, a calf can run well enough to keep up with the **herd**.

Migrating in a group helps protect the younger animals, which run in the middle of the herd. An adult wildebeest is strong enough to hurt a lion. Wildebeests can run at about 40 miles an hour (64 km/h). They will take turns sleeping and standing guard against a night attack by predators.

Icy Migrations

Some animals live in very harsh **climates**. There is not much to eat. Sometimes they must go for months without food. They store body fat to survive the hunger and cold.

The small town of Churchill, in Manitoba, Canada, lies in the middle of a polar bear migration route! Nearly 1,000 polar bears come to Churchill in the fall. Once the ice has formed, the polar bears leave to hunt seals. The bears stay on the ice, hunting and building up their body fat, until the weather warms and melting ice forces them back on land. Polar bears can then survive for six months without eating!

WOW! Floating Bear

Polar bears have been seen swimming hundreds of miles (km) from land. They may get there by floating on sheets of ice, but they can swim long distances, too.

Like polar bears, Pacific walruses follow the cold weather. They spend the winter in the Bering Sea and head north in the summer to the Chukchi Sea. Walruses migrate mainly by swimming, but they may also ride ice floes. Their calves are born during their migration north.

Thousands of walruses migrate through the narrow Bering Strait.

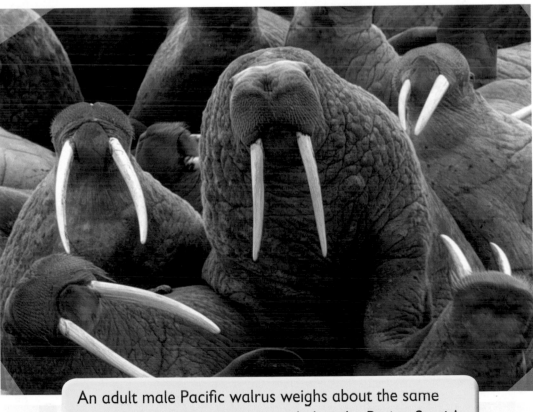

An adult male Pacific walrus weighs about the same as a family car. It can get crowded at the Bering Strait!

Difficult Journeys

There is always a good reason why animals make the amazing journeys that they do. Sometimes they need to find the ideal spot to lay their eggs.

RED CRAB MIGRATION ROAD CLOSURES

MURRAY ROAD	OPEN
SCHOOL - DRIERS	OPEN
NW POINT ROAD	OPEN
THE DALES ROAD	OPEN
WINIFRED TRACK	OPEN
CIRCUIT TRACKS	CLOSED
BLOWHOLES ROAD	OPEN
BOULDER TRACK	CLOSED
MARGARET KNOLL	OPEN
ETHEL BEACH ROAD	OPEN
GOLF COURSE ROAD	OPEN

FOR FURTHER DETAILS ON ROAD CLOSURES
PHONE 9164 8700

On Christmas Island, in the Indian Ocean, roads are closed, and special bridges and crossings are made to help the red crabs on their dangerous journey.

About 120 million red crabs do a spectacular migration from Christmas Island's forest to the coast to breed. Their eggs must be laid in the sea, but red crabs are land crabs and can't swim! They lay their eggs at a time when the tide doesn't go in or out much, so they don't drown.

On the Galápagos Islands in the Pacific Ocean, the female land iguana migrates up a steep volcano to lay her eggs! The dangerous journey takes 10 days down into the steaming **crater**. The ash in the volcano keeps the eggs warm and moist.

Marathons and Relay Races

Different insects have very different migrating habits. Some travel nonstop in their search for food. Others have a long migration that takes three or four **generations** to complete!

Ants carrying grubs to their next camp

Army ant **colonies** are always on the move. They have to move to find more food. When they travel, worker ants carry the young **grubs**. Soldier ants guard the route.

WOW! Nest of Ants

As they move, army ants build nests with their own bodies! The ants grip each other's legs and build a ball. Inside, the nest even has corridors and rooms!

Monarch butterflies have the longest insect migration, a 2,500-mile (4,000-km) loop from Mexico to Canada and back. But no single individual makes the whole round-trip! It takes three generations of butterflies to make the trip north to Canada. One super-stong generation of monarchs makes the whole journey back south to Mexico.

Female monarch butterflies lay eggs on their journey. The new generation will do the next leg.

Why do the butterflies go on such a journey? The answer is: cold weather and milkweed. Milkweed (right) is their favorite food.

Underwater Journeys

Many migrations happen underwater. Journeys don't have to be long to be amazing feats of survival. Jellyfish Lake in Palau, in the Pacific Ocean, is home to millions of jellyfish that constantly migrate around their small lake in search of sunlight.

The jellyfish got trapped in this saltwater lake about 12,000 years ago! To survive, they must follow the sun around their small lake. **Algae** growing in the jellyfish turn the sunlight into sugar, the jellyfish's food.

WOW! Around and Around

Jellyfish Lake has steep banks that make it shady. You can see the group of jellyfish avoiding the shade here.

Humpback whales live in all major oceans, spending the summer in cool waters and the winter in warmer waters. They are about 52 feet (16 m) long and weigh as much as four school buses. They eat small fish and other tiny sea animals and plants. They migrate to find new food and a safe place to have their young. During the summer, adults do not eat. They live off their layer of **blubber**.

Humpbacks travel over 3,100 miles (5,000 km) with almost no rest along the way. They travel over 1,000 miles (1,600 km) in a month.

Glossary

algae (plural of *alga*) (AL-jee)
Plantlike life forms that mostly grow in water.

blubber (BLUH-ber)
The fat of whales and other large sea mammals.

climates (KLY-muts)
The typical weather conditions of a particular region.

colonies (KAH-luh-neez)
Populations of plants or animals in a particular place that belong to one species.

crater (KRAY-tur)
A hollow, bowl-shaped opening forming the mouth of a volcano.

flyways (FLY-wayz)
Established air routes of birds that migrate.

generations (jeh-nuh-RAY-shunz)
Average lengths of time between the birth of parents and the birth of their offspring.

grazing (GRAYZ-ing)
To feed on growing grass or herbs.

grubs (GRUBZ)
Soft, thick, wormlike larvae of an insect.

herd (HURD)
A number of animals of one kind living together.

hormones (HOR-mohnz)
Body fluids that have a stimulating effect on cells.

loop (LOOP)
A curved or circle-shaped route.

migration (my-GRAY-shun)
Moving from one region or climate to another, usually on a regular schedule for feeding or breeding.

swarms (SWORMS)
Large numbers of insects grouped together and usually in motion.

wingspan (WING-span)
The distance between the tips of a pair of wings.

Websites

For web resources related to the subject of this book, go to: www.windmillbooks.com/weblinks and select this book's title.

Read More

Berkes, Marianne, and Jennifer DiRubbio. *Going Home: The Mystery of Animal Migration*. Nevada City, CA: Dawn Publications, 2010.

Carney, Elizabeth. *Great Migrations: Whales, Wildebeests, Butterflies, Elephants, and Other Amazing Animals on the Move*. Des Moines, IA: National Geographic Children's Books, 2011.

Catt, Thessaly. *Migrating with the Salmon*. Animal Journeys. New York: PowerKids Press, 2011.

Index